ANIMALS UNDER T

GREAT WHITE SHARK

IN DANGER OF EXTINCTION!

Richard Spilsbury

Heinemann LIBRARY

www.heinemann.co.uk/library
Visit our website to find out more information about **Heinemann Library** books.

To order:
☎ Phone 44 (0) 1865 888066
▤ Send a fax to 44 (0) 1865 314091
▭ Visit the Heinemann Bookshop at www.heinemann.co.uk/library to browse our catalogue and order online.

First published in Great Britain by Heinemann Library, Halley Court, Jordan Hill, Oxford OX2 8EJ, part of Harcourt Education. Heinemann is a registered trademark of Harcourt Education Ltd.

Editorial: Emma Lynch, Jilly Attwood and Claire Throp
Design: Jo Hinton-Malivoire and Tokay, Bicester, UK (www.tokay.co.uk)
Picture Research: Rosie Garai and Liz Eddison
Production: Séverine Ribierre

Originated by Ambassador Litho Ltd
Printed in China by WKT Company Limited

ISBN 0 431 18893 9
08 07 06 05 04
10 9 8 7 6 5 4 3 2 1

British Library Cataloguing in Publication Data
Spilsbury, Richard
Great White Shark - (Animals under threat)
597.3'3
A full catalogue record for this book is available from the British Library.

Acknowledgements
The Publishers would like to thank the following for permission to reproduce photographs: Ardea pp. **34** (Peter Steyn), **14**, **15**, **18**, **41** (Ralf Kiefner), **6**, **10**, **25**, **28**, **22** (Ron and Valerie Taylor), **12** (Valerie Taylor); Bruce Coleman p. **23** (Kelvin Aitken-Visual&Witte); **11** (Jim Watt), **5** (Pacific Stock); Corbis pp. **20**, **24**, **35**; Corbis pp. **26**, **32**, **39** (Jeffrey L. Rotman), **13** (Stuart Westmorland); Getty Images pp. **38** (Jeff Rotman), **9** (National Geographic/Brian Skerry); Nature Picture Library p. **21**; Nature Picture Library p. **16** (Tom Heald); NHPA pp. **33** (ANT Photolibrary), **8** (Mark Bowler), **27** (Norbert Wu), **29** (Trevor McDonald); OSF pp. **4** (David Fleetham), **31** (Howard Hall), **30** (Tobians Bernhard); PA pp. **36**, **37** (EPA); Plymouth Aquarium p. **42**; Rex/Greg Williams p. **19**; Tudor Photography p. **43**.

Cover photograph reproduced with permission of Bruce Coleman/Jim Watt.

The publishers would like to thank Dr Chris Tydeman, Environmental Consultant, for his assistance in the preparation of this book.

Contents

Words printed in the text in bold, **like this**, are explained in the Glossary.

The great white shark

Sharks are fish

All fish are **vertebrates** that live in water. Most fish swim using fins. They breathe through **gills**, their skins are covered in **scales** and they produce soft eggs. Scientists organize fish into three groups based on their skeletons: **bony fish** have hard, bony skeletons; **cartilaginous fish** have softer skeletons; and jawless fish have no jawbones. Sharks, and their close relatives the skates and rays, are types of cartilaginous fish.

The great white shark has a bad reputation. People think it will kill almost anything in the water, including them. In fact these remarkable creatures are not very well understood. A great white shark is quite picky about what it eats, and it lives a secretive life. It is also an **endangered species**. This means there are so few of them left in the oceans that they are at risk of becoming **extinct**. There is only one reason for this: people kill great whites at a faster rate than the sharks can have young, so their numbers drop.

This book is about the life of great white sharks, and why and how people kill them. It also looks at the efforts being made by some people to protect this shark and to save it from extinction.

▲ *The great white shark* (Carcharodon carcharias) *is an awesome **predator**.*

The biggest great white sharks can weigh over 3 tonnes.

The sharks

The great white is one of around 400 different species of shark. Sharks vary enormously in shape, from T-shaped hammerheads to frilly wobbegongs. They also come in many sizes, from 16 centimetre-long lanternsharks to 12 metre-long whale sharks. The great white is closely related to the mako shark. They both belong to the mackerel shark family.

Mackerel sharks all have a body shaped like a torpedo with a large tail **fin** shaped like a crescent moon. This is joined to the rest of their body by a narrow tail stalk. They have one large triangular **dorsal** (back) fin, and a second tiny dorsal fin nearer their tail. Their ten **gill slits** – five on each side – are long and wrap around the sides of their body. Mackerel sharks also have a pointed snout and large, dark eyes.

Adult great whites are the largest flesh-eating sharks. The only two larger species of shark in the world, the whale shark and the basking shark, both feed on tiny animals in the water. Great whites can grow to more than 6 metres long, but are usually nearer 4 metres. Females are generally bigger than males, but they look very similar.

Why 'great white'?

Great whites are not all white. Although they have a white belly and sides, they have a darker back in a shade of grey or olive. There are no white sharks, yet most people call them 'great' whites because of their size and power. Some other names for the great white include white pointer, maneater, jaws and white death!

Where do great white sharks live?

Nearly all **species** of shark spend their whole life in seawater. Most kinds of shark live only in **tropical** waters. Here the water remains at a similar warm temperature all year around. However, great white sharks live mostly in cooler waters between 13 °C and 20 °C. These cooler waters are where most of their **prey** lives.

Great whites live in and move between oceans all around the world. However, there are more of them in the waters around southern Africa from Namibia to South Africa, southern Australia, Japan, northeastern and southwestern USA and in the southern Mediterranean. Individual sharks sometimes stick around favourite haunts. In one Australian population, about one third of the sharks stayed around the same place throughout the year.

The right temperature

Sharks, like all fish, are **cold-blooded**. This means that the temperature of their bodies is usually the same as the water around them. Different sharks have adapted to live at different temperatures. So if, for example, a tropical shark is put into cold water it slows down, because there is not enough warmth for it to remain active. Water temperature is affected not only by climate and season, but also by water depth, currents and **upwellings**. If great whites are found in tropical areas it is usually in **currents** or upwellings of cold water. They are often found in cool waters in areas with **subtropical** or **temperate** climates.

Most shark species live in or visit tropical waters occasionally.

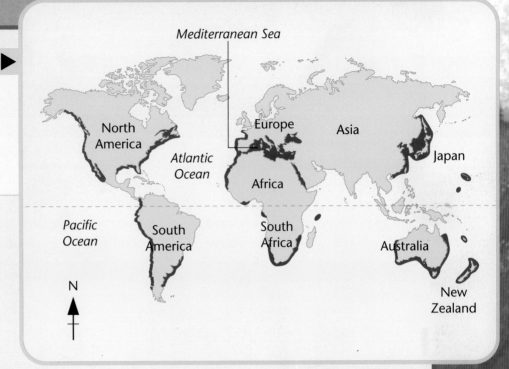

Great white sharks are often seen in the areas of ocean marked in red.

Migration

Great white sharks often **migrate** as the seasons change, to remain in water of the right temperature. They can swim a long way in a short time. For example, one large great white travelled 190 kilometres in 2.5 days.

The main reason great whites migrate is to follow their **prey**. They often target seals, which are a rich food source. The great white shark populations off the Pacific coast of the USA arrive at islands near San Francisco Bay in early April, to feed on adult fur seals. Later in April, they migrate south to islands off the coast near Los Angeles, where the seals have their babies. In May, the sharks migrate north to feed on elephant seal babies that were born in the early spring.

Depth

Great white sharks usually live in shallow water. This is because prey is more concentrated here than in the wide, deep ocean. They are found from the surfline to water depths of around 250 metres, but usually at around 20 metres. Those that live in deeper water move into shallower water, such as reefs, chains of islands and off headlands, to feed. One Australian study discovered that female great whites are more common around islands close to the coast, and males more common around islands out at sea. This is probably because shallower waters are safer places for females to have their young.

Great white shark populations

It is very difficult to count wild animals accurately. They may be very small, or spread over a wide area, or look similar. For most animals, their numbers are changing all the time as some die, others are born and some **migrate** to different areas.

Given their size, great white sharks should be quite easy to count. However, they move fast, live under water and inhabit a wide area of the world's oceans. They are not seen often at the surface, so in most cases divers would have to go down to count them. Diving is expensive, and there are obvious dangers from the sharks!

Estimating population

Scientists look at shark populations in two main ways. The first way is called capture-mark-recapture. This method assumes there is an equal chance of catching each individual shark. A number of sharks are caught and a plastic tag attached to them through their **dorsal** fin. Each tag can be individually recognized. The tagged sharks are then released. When any sharks are caught in future, the number that are tagged is recorded and used to estimate the size of the population.

When scientists tag great white sharks, they also record other information such as their size and location. When sharks are caught later the scientists can see how much they have grown and how far they have travelled.

The number of sharks seen by divers can help estimates about the total population size.

There are problems with this method. Catching a great white shark in order to tag it is very difficult, because of its size and strength. The tags sometimes fall off, and the capture of a tagged shark may not be reported to the person who tagged it.

A second way of estimating populations is based on the number of sharks caught over time by fishermen, or seen over time from boats or by divers. This gives a good idea of whether the population is getting smaller. In the 1960s, off southeastern Australia, one shark was caught on every 20 shark fishing trips in the same waters. In the 1980s, one was caught on every 650 trips. Great whites are clearly becoming much rarer there. It is now thought there could be as few as 200 great white sharks in southern Australia.

The information we have suggests that the number of great white sharks is falling worldwide. However, no-one knows exactly how many there really are in the world.

Estimating population by tagging

Imagine that 100 sharks are tagged and released, then out of 100 sharks caught later, ten have tags attached. Thus 10 per cent of the sharks caught have tags. Estimators assume that the original 100 sharks that were tagged represent 10 per cent of the total shark population. In this example, then, the population would be 1000. This is a simplified explanation. In reality scientists use more complex versions of this method to estimate populations.

The body of a great white shark

Great white sharks are superbly adapted for life in the water. All mackerel sharks have a smooth **streamlined** shape. The body of a great white shark is wide, almost circular in the middle, and tapers at either end to the pointed snout and the tail stalk.

Rough skin

Although great whites look smooth, their skin feels rough. This is because it has tiny overlapping **denticles**, or pointed **scales**. Denticles are raised on tiny stalks, unlike the flat scales on a **bony fish**. Each denticle is shaped to cut through the water. This allows the shark to swim with less effort. Points on the scales also interlock, to form tough armour. Very few animals can pierce this protective skin.

Under the skin is a layer of overlapping coils of collagen (strands of protein), a bit like rubber bands. This smoothes the great white's body – but also has another function. Giant swimming muscles inside a great white's back pull against the backbone and against the tough collagen layer. This produces very powerful swimming strokes for the amount of energy used. A great white swims using stiff flicks of its tail **fins** and tail stalk. Keels, or ridges, running along each side of the stalk help to strengthen it.

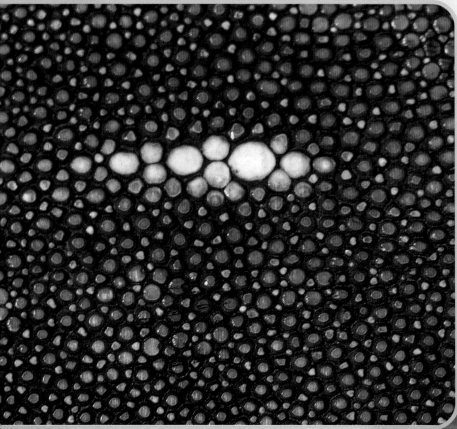

This is a close-up of the denticles on a great white's skin.

Floating and staying level

Great white sharks are heavy animals. A great white is buoyant (able to float) mostly because it has a massive liver full of oils that are lighter than water. However, this alone is not enough to stop the shark from sinking. It also has massive **pectoral** fins, which push its body upwards with the slightest swimming movement. Although the fins look rigid, great whites move them using muscles, to change the angle or speed they swim at.

Breathing under water

All fish breathe using **gills**. These are body parts with thin skin and lots of blood vessels. They transfer some of the oxygen that is dissolved in seawater to blood cells. These transport the oxygen to different parts of the body. They also transfer waste carbon dioxide from the body to the water.

As a great white swims, water is forced into its mouth, across its gills and out of its **gill slits**. However, it can also breathe for shorter periods by pumping water into its mouth and across its gills using its throat muscles.

You can see this great white's gills in passages behind its throat.

gills

Light skeleton

Sharks are also buoyant because their skeletons are light, made of **cartilage**, or gristle. Cartilage is usually bendy, but the cartilage in the parts of a shark that need to be especially strong, such as the jaws and backbone, is rigid and hard.

Staying active

Great white sharks cruise over long distances through the world's cooler oceans, in search of the **prey** that lives there. Most sharks slow down in colder waters, because the low temperature gives them less energy for activity. Great whites and other mackerel sharks, however, can stay active because although they are **cold-blooded**, they are also warm-bodied.

Warm-bodied not warm-blooded

Warm-blooded animals, such as **mammals**, maintain a constant internal temperature whatever the temperature of their surroundings. The advantage of this is that their life processes can always happen at the same rate, wherever they are. The disadvantage is that it takes a lot of energy to keep this constant temperature, so warm-blooded animals usually need to eat much more for their size than cold-blooded animals.

Warm-bodied sharks have the advantages of warm-blooded animals without needing to eat as much, although they do eat more than other types of shark. Great whites can raise their internal temperature by up to 13 °C, but only in the parts of their body that are vital for swimming and finding prey. Raised temperatures in the swimming muscles, brain and intestines make them work more efficiently.

Great white sharks can swim for longer and faster in cold water than most other sharks. They can also spot and catch prey more quickly.

Great white sharks produce a lot of muscle power by re-using the internal heat they make.

Special plumbing

When we run, we create excess heat in our muscles. To stop us overheating, heated blood moves to the surface near our skin, where it cools as it loses heat into the air. Heat is lost more quickly in cold air than in warm air. As great whites swim in cool water, they could lose heat quickly. However, they have a special circulation system that prevents this happening. This is a complex network of blood vessels called a *rete mirabile* (pronounced 'reet meerahbeelay').

Energy efficiency

A 10 °C rise in a shark's internal temperature can give it three times greater speed and strength, and faster digestion of food.

Size for size, great whites need to eat ten times more food than most other sharks.

A meal of 30 kilograms of whale blubber, or fat, can provide enough energy for a great white shark for six weeks. In this time it can swim up to 6000 kilometres!

In the *rete*, hot blood from the shark's swimming muscles moves through small **veins** very close to small **arteries** that contain oxygen-rich, cold blood from their cold heart and **gills**. Heat transfers from the veins to the arteries, warming up the cold blood. This warmed blood then moves back to the swimming muscles, intestines and brain. These parts work more efficiently because they operate with pre-warmed blood.

Great white shark teeth and jaws

The teeth and jaws of the great white shark are among the most feared in the animal kingdom. This **predator**'s success in catching food depends on its teeth being sharp at all times.

A shark may produce tens of thousands of teeth in its lifetime. Each tooth lasts around three months.

Teeth conveyor belt

A great white shark has 100–150 teeth at any one time. They are triangular with jagged edges, designed to cut and saw flesh. The teeth nearest the front of the jaw are the biggest. The teeth get gradually smaller towards the corners where the jaws meet. The upper teeth are broader and more curved than the lower teeth. Each tooth is strengthened inside with layers of **minerals**.

Shark teeth are not set firm in sockets in the jaws, like human teeth. Instead they grow from a special membrane. This membrane slowly and continually unfurls from inside the jaw **cartilage**, a bit like a toothy conveyor belt. The teeth are arranged in two or three parallel rows, following the line of the jaw. The newest teeth are folded on the inside, the oldest are standing up on the outside. As an old tooth becomes blunt or dislodged as the shark bites, a newer tooth, already formed, moves forward from the row behind to take its place. Each new tooth is slightly bigger than the preceding one, so they grow in size as the shark's body grows.

Loose jaws

As in other sharks, a great white's mouth is under its snout. This might cause a problem when it bites **prey**, as it might have to manoeuvre its body to bring its mouth forwards. However, great whites have a special adaptation that solves this problem. They have loose, sliding jaws.

As a great white opens its lower jaw to bite, its snout bends upwards. Then the upper jaw slides forwards and down, along a special groove on the skull. This makes the jaws reach further forward. As the jaws widen, cartilage behind them moves into place to hold them firm, so they can close together without slipping. The jaws clamp teeth into the prey, the snout lowers and the upper jaw slides back into place. This process is completed within two seconds.

As the shark bites, its eyes roll back into their sockets, so they look white. This protects the eyes from damage caused by prey thrashing in the water. Finally the shark shakes its head from side to side, causing its upper teeth to cut away the prey's flesh.

A great white's jaws are massive, over half a metre wide in the largest individuals. Although the jaws are made of cartilage, they can bite with a force of around 3 tonnes per square centimetre.

A supreme hunter

Adult great white sharks are **apex predators**. This means they are at the top of the **food chain**, and have no natural predators where they live. The only other large predators in the oceans are whales such as **orcas**.

Great white sharks eat a wide range of **prey**. When they are young, they eat mostly small sharks and **bony fish**, such as halibut, but also crabs and squid. As they get bigger they eat larger, faster fish, such as tuna, swordfish and barracuda, as well as small prey. They also sometimes eat marine turtles, penguins and starfish.

Saving effort

Sharks, like most predators, prefer to catch an easy meal. Great whites often eat dead whales they are attracted to by the stench of rotting flesh. They also eat fish, such as tuna, caught on **long-lines**. When hunting prey, they often target the weakest or sickest animals in a group, as these are easier to catch.

Fatty food

As they get bigger, great whites also eat marine **mammals** such as sea lions, seals, whales and dolphins. These often take a lot of effort to catch. They are agile, powerful swimmers, and often live in big groups so they can warn each other of a shark's approach. However, they are rich in **nutrients** and fat, which is contained in the thick blubber that keeps them warm in cold water. Great whites have large livers and intestines that allow them to digest this fatty food fairly quickly.

◄ Great whites occasionally leap clear of the water in pursuit of fast prey such as sea lions.

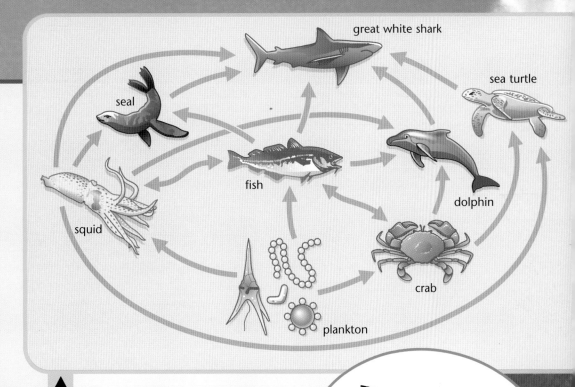

great white shark

sea turtle

seal

fish

dolphin

squid

crab

plankton

▲ *This food web gives an idea of the interdependency of great whites and other organisms in their ocean habitat.*

Getting a meal

Great white sharks usually hunt by ambush. They keep out of sight of prey by moving through the shadows, close to rocks. They have dark upper sides that cannot easily be seen by prey above them in the water, as they look down towards darker water. They also have a white underside that cannot easily be seen by prey from below, looking up into lighter water. This is called countershading.

When a great white has spotted a victim, it swims towards it in a short, high-speed burst. The force of this sometimes knocks the prey clear of the water. Great whites usually attack from below, but different prey are handled slightly differently. For example, with large elephant seals they attack the head, neck or rear flippers, and then swim away. Their bite causes massive blood loss in the seal. The shark moves in to eat this potentially dangerous prey once it has bled to death. Smaller prey, such as seals, are often caught in the shark's jaws and dragged under water until they drown.

A shark's hunting success improves with experience. In the sea off California, USA, experienced great whites stay close to colonies of elephant seals at high tide. They know that the beaches where the seals gather get very crowded at high tide, so more seals will enter the water.

Great white shark senses

Great white sharks, like other animals, use a range of senses to understand and react to the world around them.

Smell

Sharks can smell amazingly well. They can detect smells as weak as ten drops of blood in a swimming pool. As they swim, water flows into their nostrils where special sacs detect any scents. They are especially sensitive to smells associated with food such as blood from injured **prey**. Once they have sensed a smell, they swim around until they can locate where it is strongest, then move towards it, usually along ocean **currents**. Sometimes sharks stick their noses out of the water to smell the air and find out where prey are, for example to find a colony of sea lions on land.

Sight

Great whites have large eyes that are very sensitive to movement and contrast (light and dark) within a range of 25 metres. This is vital in tracking prey or other sharks, and judging their size as they get closer. Shark eyes work ten times better than ours in low light conditions, because they have a special reflective **retina**. This bounces any available light – even the dim light from stars – towards the most sensitive parts of the eye. When sharks see in daylight, the **iris** closes to protect these sensitive parts.

Unlike any other fish, great white sharks raise their head out of the water to see and smell above the surface.

Bite test

Sharks feel things using their teeth. Shark teeth are full of nerves that can sense hardness. Sensitive pores in their mouth can taste. When great whites approach unfamiliar objects, such as buoys, they often bite them. This is not to cause damage, but to find out what they are.

Hearing and feeling

Sounds travel under water as vibrations (wobbles) in the water. Sharks detect these vibrations in two ways. They partly use ears inside their skull, connected to the outside by two pores (little holes) behind their eyes. They mainly use their **lateral lines**, a row of pores along each side. Vibrations in the water move fluid trapped behind the pores. Vibrations in the fluid move tiny sensitive hairs. The lateral lines allow a shark to sense vibrations all around its body, not just on its head. Sharks are especially sensitive to the movements of struggling or injured prey.

▲ *This great white shark is finding out about an unfamiliar buoy by biting it.*

The sixth sense

In addition to sight, smell, hearing, touch and taste, sharks have a sixth sense, called **electroreception**. All living things produce weak electrical signals. These signals travel well through water. Great whites have pores dotted over their snout, called **ampullae**. These are full of a jelly-like substance that is attached to nerves that pass information to the brain. The 'jelly' conducts even tiny amounts of electricity in the water to the nerves. As well as detecting electricity caused by prey movements, great whites can also detect the Earth's **magnetic field**. So their ampullae help them to find their way around as they move through the oceans.

Great white shark society

Great white sharks are usually thought of as solitary killers roaming the oceans. In fact, they are much more social animals than we imagine. They may gather in large numbers where there is lots of food.

Dominance

When a number of great whites come together, particularly at feeding sites, there will be some that feed first or that the others steer clear of. These are the dominant individuals, the ones the others consider most important. Dominant sharks are usually the biggest, and therefore probably the strongest and most dangerous. There are further levels of importance within the group, based on size.

If two great whites approach each other, they turn away at the same time and sometimes swim in parallel. Each is seeing how big the other one is, to work out its place in the group.

Avoiding fights

When they are competing for the same **prey**, or at breeding time, great whites feel threatened if others come too close. Their jaws and teeth can kill or seriously injure other great whites that threaten them. However, they rarely fight because they risk being badly injured themselves. Instead, sharks behave in special ways to communicate their feelings.

Great whites interact with other great whites in different, usually peaceful, ways.

A great white shark often slaps the water or other sharks with its strong tail.

Snarling

A great white shark that feels threatened **displays** by swimming in an unusually stiff position, with its back hunched and **pectoral fins** held pointing downward. It even does this while swimming upside down. Stiff-swimming is often combined with opening its mouth, sliding forward its upper jaw and displaying its teeth. This delivers a clear message: 'I have sharp teeth I could use on you if I wanted!' If these displays do not deter another shark, great whites will attack. They try not to injure each other badly at first. They slam their bodies together, or slap each other with their tail fins. These shows of strength usually confirm who is the strongest and most dominant, and serious fighting is avoided. However, more damaging fights can happen during breeding season, when rival males may compete for the same female.

Biting

Great whites, especially youngsters, sometimes bump, bite and then release each other. Just as they test objects and other animals to see if they are good to eat, they test each other to get to know each other. Adult males and females also bite each other when they get close at breeding time. Great whites are protected by their tough **denticles**, and rapidly healing skin, but many have scars on their bodies not only from struggling prey, but also from other great whites.

Great white shark breeding

We do not know all the details about how great white sharks breed, or produce young. It is thought that they gather together in particular areas of warmer, shallower water to breed. Areas where many baby great whites have been caught by fishermen include the Sicilian channel in the Mediterranean Sea (between Sicily and Tunisia), and the Pacific Ocean off southern California, USA.

Mating and eggs

All male sharks mate using two claspers. Claspers are folds of skin with grooves, next to the **pelvic fins**. When two sharks mate, the male often grasps the female's **pectoral** fin to hold her close. His sperm moves along the groove of one clasper inside the female and fertilizes her eggs. (In most other fish the female's eggs are fertilized outside her body, when the male sheds his sperm on to them.) Once they have mated, males leave the females.

The fertilized eggs take around a year to fully develop inside a female. There are usually between five and ten fertilized eggs, sometimes more. As the **embryos** develop, they feed at first on the yolk in their eggs. Part of the yolk attaches to their mother's body and taps into her blood. This gives the embryos **nutrients** and oxygen. As the embryos get bigger, they also feed on unfertilized eggs, smaller embryos and their own shed teeth, which provide them with extra **minerals**.

You can see the claspers on the underside of this male great white.

Birth and growth

Like most sharks, great whites give birth to live pups (babies), instead of laying eggs. The pups hatch out of the eggs inside the mother, and are then born. Female great whites give birth to two to ten pups. Newborn pups are 1.2–1.5 metres long, and are just like their parents. They can swim powerfully and catch their own food as soon as they are born.

Great white pups grow slowly, although they grow more quickly in warmer waters than cold. Females take 10–14 years to reach 5 metres, the usual size when they become able to breed themselves. Males take 9–10 years to reach maturity.

Pros and cons of live birth

One of the advantages for sharks of keeping their babies safe inside for longer is that the pups are developed enough to fend for themselves when they are born. This makes them more likely to survive, and reproduce themselves in the future. However, as each pup takes up room inside its mother, not many can be produced at one time. Fish that lay lots of small eggs that develop outside their body can have many more young. Another disadvantage is that developing pups use up a female's valuable nutrients, so she has to feed more often while pregnant. A great white female may need a year between giving birth and mating again, to build up enough food reserves to be able to bear young.

▲ The great white pups are born in spring to late summer, in warm water.

Young great white sharks face a few **predators** in the wild, including other, larger sharks. For an adult great white, the only natural threat is from a group of hunting **orca** whales. Even so, far fewer great whites are killed by orcas than are killed by people.

People are not much of a match for great white sharks – we are much smaller and weaker, and equipped only with small teeth. We can only take on great whites because we have developed effective weapons and tools, and ways of working together. People kill great whites because they think sharks are dangerous, and because they can be sold for money. We also kill them by accident as we fish for other **species**, or by destroying their **habitats**.

Increasing danger

All sharks are increasingly in danger because of the rapidly rising human population. As more people demand more food, fishing vessels try to catch more fish, including sharks. There are fewer fish to catch, so to make a living the fishermen target more valuable species, regardless of how rare or **endangered** they may be.

More and more people today live by and visit coasts. They do this because of the scenery and **climate**, the jobs available there, such as fishing and tourism, and because of the lifestyle. Many people visit coasts for watersports, from swimming and boating to diving and surfing.

A person paddling on a surfboard could look like a seal or whale to a great white swimming below.

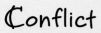

This man survived being bitten by a great white because it was not really trying to hurt him.

Conflict

The more people there are in the water, the more likely it is that some will come across a potentially dangerous creature such as a great white shark. Great whites will hunt any **prey** they find in the sea, and this occasionally includes people. They have a reputation as regular maneaters, but although they are one of the most likely shark species to target people, encounters and fatal attacks are surprisingly rare.

It is likely that great whites attack people mostly because of mistaken identity. The most frequent victims are surfers. To a shark swimming below them, a person paddling on a surfboard may look like a small shark, whale or seal. Great whites test unknown things using their teeth, and in most attacks their bites injure but do not remove flesh, which they easily could if they wanted to. This may be because a person is not such good eating as a fat seal or whale!

Shark fishing

For centuries fishermen have tried to catch many kinds of shark, both to eat them and to remove a dangerous creature from the sea. In the last 80 years, they have had a new motive – trophy hunting. Some people like to show off sharks' teeth or the whole jaw, to prove they are expert hunters.

Great white shark jaws are sought-after trophies around the world.

Trophy hunters

Shark trophy hunting became popular in the 1920s in the seas off Australia, South Africa and the USA. People wanted to show that they could conquer wild beasts, not only big game on land – such as tigers in Asia – but also big fish in the oceans. They tried to catch the biggest, most aggressive fish they could find such as great whites. They used strong rods and reels.

In the seas off Australia and South Africa in the 1950s, fishermen began to make shark fishing easier. They lured great whites to an area by throwing buckets of fish blood, oil and guts into the water. This is called **chumming**. The sharks were then hooked at the surface using harpoons, or shot from boats. As a souvenir, and to prove they really had caught a great white, the fishermen would have their photos taken back on shore, with the shark strung up from weighing scales.

The hunt for great whites increased in intensity in the 1980s, following the success of a book and film called *Jaws*. More collectors wanted teeth and well-preserved jaws to show off, without having taken part in the chase. Shark hunters, keen to cash in on this interest, now caught sharks more often using easier methods. For example, they would poison chunks of fish and attach them to thick chains that hung down in the water from empty oil-drums. Since the 1990s, trade in shark jaws has increased as more people sell and buy over the Internet. A large set of great white shark jaws recently fetched $50,000.

Flesh and fins

People also still catch and sell sharks to eat. Great white shark meat is eaten fresh, dried, salted or smoked. Oil is extracted from its liver and sold as a vitamin supplement to fight colds. However, by far the greatest demand is for the **fins** of many sharks, including great whites. Their **cartilage**-rich fins are traditionally used in Chinese cookery to make a thick soup. In the past, shark's fin soup was an expensive luxury. But wealth increased in China in the 1980s, so more people could afford shark's fin products. This was when shark fishing expanded massively all over the world. The majority of sharks caught today are **finned**. This means that their fins are cut off, and their still living bodies are thrown back into the water to die.

Today, fishermen sell a kilogram of shark's fin for around £8. In a restaurant a single bowl of shark's fin soup costs around £70.

The accidental killing of sharks

Trophy hunting for great whites only contributes a small amount to the decrease in their numbers. The biggest cause of death for sharks of all **species** is **bycatch**. Bycatch is when fishermen catch something accidentally while trying to catch something else. Many **threatened** sea creatures are at risk from bycatch, because of the enormous scale of commercial fishing around the world.

Overfishing

Today, fishing vessels catch so many fish that around 70 per cent of all species caught for food are being overfished. This means we are removing far more fish from populations than are being added as a result of breeding. In some areas, once common fish, such as cod and anchovy, are now rare, because of overfishing.

Bycatch of sharks happens for various reasons. It is usually because the sharks are hunting the fish, or fish-eating **predators**, such as dolphins, that people are trying to catch. Massive ships, sometimes working in pairs, drag immense nets through the oceans, catching any fish they can, regardless of their size or rarity. If sharks are caught in nets they usually drown, because water cannot pass over their **gills** fast enough for them to breathe. Other sharks are caught on the numerous baited hooks on **long-lines** trailing off tuna ships, or when they eat already hooked tuna.

Sharks, such as great whites, may get caught accidentally on fishing nets and die.

These people are checking a shark net that protects swimmers off the South African coast.

In the past, shark bycatch was usually thrown back into the sea, because the price sharks could fetch at market was too low to justify the amount of space their bodies would take up onboard. Now that their **fins** are so valuable, the sharks are usually **finned** before being discarded.

Shark nets

Sharks are also killed accidentally on shark nets. These strong nets are strung offshore from certain popular beaches and bays, to keep people and sharks apart. Sharks, dolphins and other marine animals often get tangled in them, and drown or starve to death.

Destroying great white shark habitats

▲ This dead coral was dislodged by bottom trawls. What was once a rich reef habitat is now barren.

We are destroying ocean **habitats**, just as we are destroying habitats on land. Under water, however, a lot of the destruction is hidden from view. When marine habitats are destroyed it affects some **species** more than others, but all are affected because whole **ecosystems** are disturbed. For example, although a **predator**, such as the great white shark, may not be affected directly, it will be affected if there is less **prey** for it to eat.

Destroying the ocean floor

Great white shark populations can suffer badly in areas where the ocean floor is destroyed. For example, along the coast of California, USA, over 80 per cent of fish species once thought to be common, including the great white shark, are now considered rare. The great white is among these partly because its favoured prey, such as rockfish, are becoming rare.

The ocean floor is mainly destroyed by a method of fishing that uses bottom trawls. These are wide nets, weighed down with heavy rollers, that are pulled by trawlers across the ocean floor. They are so strong they knock over or sweep up everything they hit. One pass of a bottom trawl can ruin large areas of coastal coral and seagrass that have taken years to establish. These provide shelter and breeding grounds for complex ecosystems of marine creatures such as fish, starfish, crabs and sponges. These in turn feed larger fish, sea lions and **apex predators** such as great white sharks.

'The way we fish is like hanging a huge net dragged from an airship across a forest, knocking down the trees and scooping up the plants and animals, and then throwing away everything except the deer.'
Elliott Norse, biologist

The Mediterranean Sea is highly polluted. This has affected populations of dolphins, monk seals and many species of fish. Fewer great white sharks are caught by trawlers, partly because of this effect on their prey.

Pollution and development

Some coastal pollution happens as a result of development. For example, governments may encourage tourism in coastal areas because it creates jobs. However, the pollution produced by tourists may ruin local fishing industries.

Pollution

We treat the oceans like a massive waste bin. Some of our pollution sinks or disperses, but most sticks around and affects marine life. Most pollution comes from land. Sewage, sludge, oil, fertilizers and industrial waste are washed off land or dumped into drains and rivers. Other pollution, such as radioactive waste, rubbish and oil washed out of oil tankers, is dumped at sea.

Great white sharks are rarely affected directly by pollution. However, pollutants may affect their prey. For example, fertilizers make marine plants called algae grow so much that they cut out light to the sea floor, killing other algae below. When bacteria break down these algae, they use up so much oxygen in the water that fewer fish can survive there. This means fewer prey for small predators and, through the **food chain**, for sharks.

Dealing with fishing

The number of great white sharks in places where they were once abundant has dropped considerably, because of the wide range of serious threats they face. Logbooks kept by **long-line** tuna fishing boats, for example, have recorded an 80 per cent drop in great white sharks caught as **bycatch** in certain areas. Still, no-one knows for certain what the total population once was and what it is now, so a drop in one area may simply mean that great whites have moved on and are now abundant in other areas.

However, if great white populations have dropped, they will take a long time to recover because these animals take a long time to grow and mature, and because they bear few young. Given this, several countries have taken bold steps to protect the remaining great whites around their coasts. These countries took action because people demanded that more should be done to **conserve** great white sharks.

Protecting great whites using laws

The first country to protect great white sharks using the law was South Africa. In 1991, it banned the killing, injuring or sale of great whites or any great white products such as **fins**. If anyone breaks these laws, they risk heavy fines, having their boat confiscated or even a jail sentence. Nearby Namibia followed South Africa's lead in 1993.

Legal protection for great whites in parts of the USA started in 1994. A California State Assembly Bill prevented the development of commercial great white fishing activities along its coasts. Populations of great whites in Atlantic US waters were officially protected from 1997.

This massive shark was caught illegally in Sicily.

Today, in California, USA, the only legal capture of great whites is as bycatch from approved commercial fishing vessels, and by scientists who have capture permits.

In Australia, scientists first proposed in 1995 that **chumming** should be banned close to the coast, and that fishing hooks should be restricted in size – great whites can only be caught using especially big hooks. They also insisted that shark-cage tourist operators must have a licence to run their businesses. The Australian government made this law in 1997, when the great white shark was officially described as **endangered** and given the protection it needs.

Honesty motivation

Given the protected status of great whites in certain countries, many fishing vessels are reluctant to admit to bycatch. Several governments are offering encouragements, such as money, to fishing vessels who tag and release, rather than kill, sharks or leave them to die. Tags can contain sensitive equipment that records how deep sharks dive and how far they swim, and can track their movements. In this way, conservation scientists can help understand the journeys of great whites through the oceans. Governments can then use this knowledge to improve the protection of great whites.

Illegal chumming was used to entice this great white to take the bait and become hooked.

Saving great white shark ecosystems

The laws made to help **conserve** great white sharks are an important step. However, they only apply to some areas where great whites live, and they do not limit **bycatch**, pollution or fishing practices that destroy marine **habitat**. Nevertheless, there are practical ways in which people can help save shark **ecosystems**.

*It takes a lot of time and money to clean up pollution. **Currents** and waves can spread pollution over a wide area. This oil spill was a result of MV Treasure sinking at Cape Town in 2000.*

Marine reserves

Marine reserves are areas where fishing is banned or closely controlled by wardens (guards). Access is only allowed if boats or divers have permits. Reserves allow large numbers of fish, including sharks, to gather and breed. It is hoped that their young will restock the adjoining areas. Unlike many land reserves, marine reserves do not have fences around them, so fish and other marine animals come and go. Like any reserves, the larger the area the more expensive it is to maintain, with more wardens and equipment. Marine reserves have been set up around Dyer Island off South Africa, and the Farallon Islands off California, to conserve great white sharks in particular. Many more reserves have been set up around the world, dedicated to conserving rich ecosystems of marine life, including coral reefs where many different shark **species** live.

▲ Greenpeace, an international conservation group, running a campaign encouraging countries to protect endangered toothfish, which are victims of pirate fishing.

Changing the fishing industry

It is possible to control fishing to the benefit of great white sharks and other **threatened** marine creatures, and to the people who fish. For example, fishing vessels can reduce bycatch and save marine habitat by not fishing with destructive bottom trawls. Although their catches will be smaller in the short term in the waters around those areas, over a longer period the ecosystem will remain healthy. This means fishing can become sustainable – fish can be harvested from the same waters year after year, without their numbers falling.

Many governments make laws to control wasteful bycatch. However, these laws are useless unless they are enforced. To enforce them, government observers need to be on board trawlers to monitor the amount of fish caught and the bycatch. They fine the people who own the boats if catches exceed agreed limits.

stopping pirate fishing

Pirate fishing is a major problem for governments trying to control fishing in their waters. Governments usually control how much fish a boat from its own country can catch and where it can fish. However, it cannot control boats from other countries. Pirate vessels fish where they please and take as much as they want, including **endangered** and threatened marine animals. They are difficult to stop because they carefully hide their owners' identities by regularly changing names and crews. They always fly 'flags of convenience'. This means they pay money to register with a country that does not enforce fishing restrictions such as Belize or Honduras.

Conservation efforts

Fishing creates jobs for millions of people around the world. Governments are often reluctant to control fishing, because it might affect jobs and make the government unpopular. It is also expensive to control fishing, and poorer countries may not have the funds to do it effectively. Governments are more likely to control fishing if members of the public and **conservation** groups encourage them.

Conservation groups

There are many local, national and international conservation groups dedicated to conserving sharks and marine life in general. Many are non-governmental organizations (NGOs) such as WWF and Greenpeace. NGOs raise money for conservation from donations by the public and businesses. They raise public awareness of the dangers to all sharks, using advertising campaigns and fundraising events. They also sometimes take more direct action, such as revealing the identities of pirate fishing vessel owners, or obstructing shark killing.

Specialist shark scientists employed by NGOs often advise governments on how best to improve conservation. The International Union for Conservation of Nature and Natural Resources (IUCN) is an international group that has a Shark Specialist Group, which combines government and NGO scientific expertise. The Group makes recommendations to governments worldwide on how best to control shark fishing, and where to create **marine reserves**. It also campaigns with other groups to make **finning** illegal.

Undercover conservation workers discovered this shop in Hong Kong full of shark fins, mostly supplied by illegal finning.

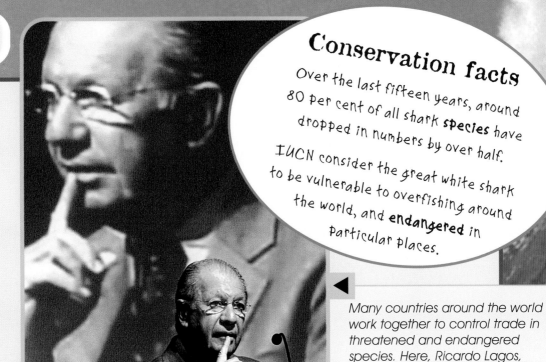

Many countries around the world work together to control trade in threatened and endangered species. Here, Ricardo Lagos, President of Chile, represents his country in the 12th CITES Convention in 2002.

Acting internationally

Great white sharks travel long distances. This means that although local conservation laws are vital, they can only be effective if they extend into national and international waters. For example, great whites are partly protected in the important breeding area of the Sicilian Channel in the Mediterranean Sea, but once they enter Tunisian waters they are unprotected.

Trade in shark trophies and **fins** between countries is controlled and regulated by the Convention on International Trade in Endangered Species of Wild Fauna and Flora (CITES, pronounced 'sightease'). They work in cooperation with customs and police officers around the world, to prevent the illegal smuggling of shark parts.

Consumer power

Despite the conservation measures aimed at fishing methods, large-scale shark killing will continue as long as people want to buy shark meat and fins, jaws and teeth. WWF has helped to set up the Marine Stewardship Council, to encourage shoppers only to buy legally caught fish and fish products that are labelled. An example of this approach is the labelling of dolphin-friendly tuna. However, although the **long-lines** catch fewer dolphins than the large nets of the past, they still catch many sharks.

Great white shark tourism

Coming face to face with a great white shark is many people's worst nightmare. However, a surprising number of people are happy to pay for the chance to get up close. There are advantages and disadvantages for great whites in these encounters.

Getting too chummy

In the early days of tourist cage diving in Australia, in the 1980s, tourist companies offered pay-for-view trips – if no shark showed, they did not get paid. So, many started to chum. Excessive chumming, as happened off California in the USA in the 1990s, attracted lots of sharks, but it also increased shark attacks on local surfers and divers, because the sharks learnt to associate people with food! Another result of this association is that great whites in certain areas will approach boats. Shark hunters in boats can then easily kill them.

Getting closer

Tourists, whether daytrippers, scientists or film-makers, get close to great whites by taking boat trips to known shark locations such as Dyer Island off South Africa and Dangerous Reef in Australia. Some tourists watch sharks when they rise to the surface to feed. Others in wetsuits and **SCUBA** kit are lowered under the waves in large, reinforced cages. The sharks approach cages and boats out of curiosity, but also because people lure them to the area by **chumming**.

Steel shark cages float just at the surface. The divers inside are closely examined by the sharks.

Shark tourist boats should use enough chum to attract great whites, but not feed them, as this may encourage attacks on people.

Helpful tourism

Shark tourism can have positive effects. Some money from shark tourism, from visitors' tickets, cage permits and items such as posters and T-shirts, goes directly to **marine reserves** and **conservation** groups. Some goes to private cage operators. Visitors also learn more about great whites, and are more likely to support shark conservation in the future.

Several conservation groups run their own shark tourism ventures. South Africa's White Shark Research Institute does this. Tourists pay or volunteer to become shark scientists for a while. They may photograph and film sharks to recognize individuals by markings and **fin** shape, and make observations about their behaviour.

The other side of tourism

Any tourist venture where people see protected animals in the wild raises a difficult question: how do you let enough people get close in order to make money, without affecting the animals and their **ecosystem**? More tourists in an area may mean more litter, sewage and other pollution. Noise from lots of boats and cages jostling for position in shark alley – the best great white spotting place off Dyer Island – for example, may disturb other animals such as fur seals, whales and seabirds.

The future for great white sharks

By 2003, great white sharks were legally protected in only a few countries. Their long-term survival can only be achieved by international laws, enforced consistently by countries all over the world.

CITES listing

The Australian government, backed by a variety of **conservation** groups, is trying to get the great white shark listed by CITES. CITES keep two lists of **threatened** and **endangered** animals. Those in Appendix I risk **extinction** without lots of protection, and those in Appendix II need to be closely monitored because they are threatened. CITES listing for great whites has been slow to come since it was first suggested in 1998, because although reductions in great white **bycatch** suggest falling populations, actual population sizes are not known. It is not certain whether the great white shark is rare or not, but listing would create a basis for shark protection worldwide.

Recent advances in great white shark study

People who study great whites learn new things about them every year. Here are just two recent findings.

· *Regional variation*
In different places great whites look different. Californian sharks have dark grey backs and thin bodies. South African sharks have fawn or olive backs and fatter bodies. This suggests there are distinct populations in the Atlantic and Pacific Oceans.

· *Electrical defence*
In future, people who spend time in great white waters, such as divers and surfers, will be able to repel sharks. Protective Oceanic Devices, or PODs, create an electrical field that irritates the **ampullae** on a shark's snout, making it swim away. They can also be put on offshore shark nets and fishermen's **long-lines**, to protect the sharks.

The future for great white sharks is extremely uncertain.

Knowing more

We know little about many aspects of the great white shark's life. Many more years of observation and monitoring by scientists are needed to better understand them. We know they are slow to grow and reproduce, so will always be vulnerable to threats from people. It is important to find out where exactly in the world's oceans they breed. Then we will know which areas we must protect.

What we do know is that great whites are being killed in great numbers. If we do not protect them now, these awesome animals may well be lost to future generations.

Breeding sharks in captivity?

When wild populations of some **species** are low, captive breeding programmes in sanctuaries can restock the wild. This has proved suitable for animals such as American alligators. However, great white sharks have never survived long in captivity, and do not breed there. There are several problems. Great whites are wide-ranging **predators** that need a lot of food and space to survive. They do not get this in captivity. Also, the weak electrical fields created by equipment in aquariums disorientate great whites' **electroreception**, severely affecting how they sense their surroundings. Breeding in captivity will only become possible if we can learn more about these creatures.

How can you help?

It may be difficult to imagine how you can help great white sharks, but there are some simple things you can do to make a difference to their lives. The important thing to remember is that the people who make laws around the world protecting sharks, mostly listen to the opinions of ordinary people just like you.

Learn about shark conservation

The more you know about the problems facing sharks, the more effectively you can join in helping them. So read books, watch documentaries or visit some of the many websites devoted to sharks (see pages 46–7 for details). You may be lucky enough to visit a local museum, zoo or aquarium with a shark exhibit, or even go on a shark-watching trip. Once you know more about the scale of **finning**, for example, you can tell your friends and family. You could even suggest sharks as a school study topic.

Get writing

You need to tell decision makers how you feel about the numbers of sharks being killed. There are several good ways to do this. You can add your signature to an existing petition (a letter whose thoughts you agree with) started by a **conservation** group. In Autumn 2000 the US government were debating whether to ban finning in US waters. WWF organized 18,000 messages in support of the Shark Finning Prohibition Act. These messages encouraged the Act to be made law.

Although aquariums will not have live great white sharks, they are good places to learn more about all types of shark. This is a model great white recently displayed in an aquarium.

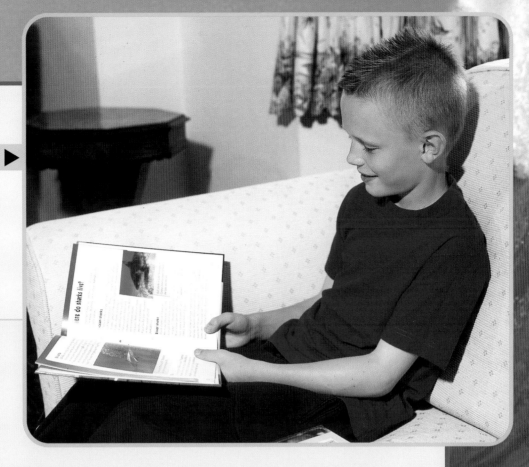

▶ *Know your subject by reading as much as you can about sharks.*

Write your own letters demanding a change in the way great white sharks are treated. Many shark conservation groups, such as SharkResearch in Australia, can provide help on wording a letter so it has most impact. Letters like this can then be used in a variety of ways. You could start your own petition and ask local shops, schools and libraries for space to leave it for others to sign. You could send a letter direct to your government, state representative or leader. You could write to your local or national newspapers.

Buy carefully

The shark killing industry is encouraged by demand. Encourage others to avoid all shark products. For example, do not eat at restaurants that serve shark's **fin** soup, and tell them why you will not. Never buy shark trophies such as teeth and jawbones.

Donate

Not all of us have much money to donate to shark conservation groups, so encourage others to give a little bit each. You can do this by taking part in a sponsored activity, or by joining with others to sponsor a shark. You could volunteer your time with shark campaigners in your local town or city, and help collect money from people in the street. If you do this, and you have learnt lots about sharks, you will also be able to answer people's questions.

Glossary

ampullae   jelly-filled pits sensitive to stimulus such as electricity

apex predator   animal that eats other animals and is so big or strong that usually no other animals kill or eat it

artery   blood vessel that transports blood cells carrying oxygen

bony fish   fish, such as cod, that have skeletons made of hard bone

bycatch   what is caught accidentally when trying to catch fish

cartilage   tough but flexible tissue containing collagen, as found in human ears or shark skeletons, for example

cartilaginous fish   fish, such as sharks, with cartilage skeletons

chumming   throwing dead fish, blood, etc. into the sea to attract other fish such as sharks

cold-blooded   animal whose body temperature changes with that of its surroundings

conservation   work people do to protect wildlife and the natural habitats of the world

current   stream of water in an ocean moving in a particular direction, often with a different temperature to the stiller water around it

denticles   shaped sharp scales

display   special behaviour, often using particular body parts or positions, with a particular meaning

dorsal   attached to or part of the back

ecosystem   community of animals and plants that interact or influence each other's lives in a particular area

electroreception   an electrical sense

embryo   unformed baby fish inside the egg

endangered   species that has so few members it is in danger of becoming extinct

extinct   when a species has died out and no longer exists

fin   flap of skin, with or without bones inside, used for swimming

finning   cutting off and keeping fins and throwing the remains of the body back into the sea

food chain   chain that shows the order in which food energy passes from plants to animals

gills   special body parts found in all fish, used to breathe underwater

gill slits   slits on cartilaginous fish where water leaves the body after passing over gills

habitat   place in the natural world where a particular organism lives

iris   part of eye that changes shape to control how much light enters

long-line   long fishing line with many hooks attached

magnetic field   pattern of magnetic force around the Earth. Many animals use it to find their way around.

mammal   warm-blooded animal with hair that can feed its young with milk from its body

marine reserve   area where fishing is banned or closely controlled

migrate   move from one place to another, often because it offers better feeding or climate

mineral   chemical, such as calcium, needed by living things

nutrients   chemicals that plants and animals need in order to live and grow well

orca   large black and white toothed whale

pectoral   attached to or part of the chest

pelvic   attached to or part of the pelvis

predator   animal that hunts and eats other animals

prey   animal that is hunted and eaten by another animal

retina   thin layer at the back of an eye that reacts to light

scale   thickened piece of dead surface skin

SCUBA   underwater breathing apparatus of air tank and mouthpiece

species   type of animal that cannot breed successfully with any other type

streamlined   shaped to move smoothly through water or air

temperate   describes areas with warm summers and cold winters

threatened   at risk of becoming endangered

tropical   warm areas of Earth north and south of the equator

upwelling   upward movement of colder water from the sea floor

vein   blood vessel that transports blood cells carrying carbon dioxide

vertebrate   animal with a backbone

Websites

Wildaid

www.wildaid.org

A site presenting a variety of **conservation** initiatives. In 2003, there was an e-petition on WildAid's website calling for shark **finning** to be banned around the world.

National Coalition for Marine Conservation

www.savethefish.org

The website of the US National Coalition for Marine Conservation, which works to conserve fish by preventing overfishing, reducing **bycatch** and protecting **habitat**.

White Shark Trust

www.whitesharktrust.org

Dedicated to great white shark conservation in South Africa and other countries. They run a support-a-shark scheme where you pay to support research into, and conservation of, great whites.

The Shark Trust

www.sharktrust.org

Based at Plymouth's National Aquarium. Lots of shark information, especially about UK and European **species**. The site also has details of how to take part in conservation studies, such as the Great Eggcase Hunt (patrolling beaches for shark and dogfish eggcases to find out about their population).

WWF

www.panda.org

WWF is a massive global organization committed to protecting the natural world. Their site contains lots of information about their conservation work for sharks and many other animals.

Greenpeace

www.greenpeace.org

Greenpeace actively campaigns to save marine **ecosystems** from overfishing, pollution and other threats.

Other shark conservation websites

www.sharkresearch.com
An Australian shark research and conservation site.

www.flmnh.ufl.edu/fish/organizations/ssg/ssg.htm
IUCN has a Shark Specialist Group, a group of specialist shark scientists who advise governments and conservation groups about shark biology and populations.

www.ea.gov.au/coasts/species/sharks/greatwhite/index.html
An Australian great white information, research and conservation site.

www.marine.csiro.au/research/tagging/neale/index.htm
This site has information about how scientists tagged a great white (they called Neale!), and what they learnt about his movements around Australia.

www.flmnh.ufl.edu/fish/sharks/isaf/isaf.htm
This University of Florida site is full of good material on shark attacks, among other things.

Books

Eyewitness: Shark, Miranda MacQuitty (Dorling Kindersley, 1992)
Great White Sharks, Marie Levine (Weigel Educational Publishers, 1998)
The Private Life of Sharks: the truth behind the myth, Michael Bright (Robson Books, 1999)
Reader's Digest Pathfinders: Sharks and Other Sea Creatures, Leighton Taylor (Reader's Digest, 2000)
Sharks, Erik D. Stoops and Sherrie Stoops (Sterling Publishing, 1994)

Videos

BBC Wildlife Special – Great White Shark, The Silent Stalker narrated by David Attenborough (BBC, 2000)
Hunt For The Great White Shark (National Geographic Videos, 1994)

Index

Titles in the *Animals Under Threat* series include:

Hardback   0 431 18892 0

Hardback   0 431 18888 2

Hardback   0 431 18889 0

Hardback   0 431 18893 9

Hardback   0 431 18890 4

Hardback   0 431 18891 2

Find out about the other titles in this series on our website www.heinemann.co.uk/library